BUSINESS-DAY TRADING

BUSINESS-DAY TRADING

STOCK OPTIONS

DUPREE E. WALKER

CONTENTS

INTRODUCTION

Creating a business in the dynamic world of day trading, every decision can lead to significant financial outcomes. First, you have the choice to trade as an individual or sole proprietor or trade through a business entity such as a limited liability company.

Day trading as a business involves buying and selling securities within the same trading day to profit from short-term price fluctuations. It's a high-risk, high-reward activity that requires significant knowledge, skill, and discipline.

INTRODUCTION TO OPTIONS TRADING

Options trading can seem complex and difficult to understand for beginners, but once you grasp the basics, it becomes a valuable tool for diversifying your investment portfolio and managing risk. Unlike traditional stocks, options give you the right, but not the obligation, to buy or sell an asset at a predetermined price within a specific period. In this book, we'll guide you through the fundamentals of options trading, from basic concepts to advanced strategies.

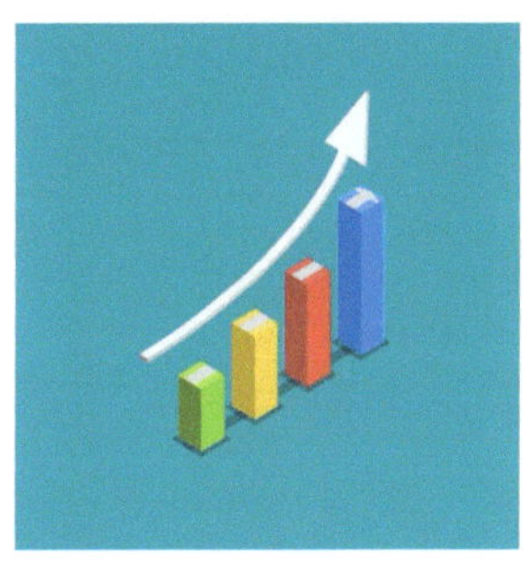

UNDERSTANDING OPTIONS

To start, let's break down what an option is. An option is a financial derivative, meaning its value is derived from the price of another asset, typically a stock.

There are two main types of options: call options and put options.

Call Options

A call option gives the holder the right to purchase the underlying asset at a specific price, known as the strike price, before the option expires. Investors buy call options when they anticipate that the price of the underlying asset will rise.

. . .

Put Options

On the other hand, a put option gives the holder the right to sell the underlying asset at the strike price before the option expires. Investors buy put options when they expect the price of the underlying asset to fall.

Key Terminology

Before diving deeper, its crucial to understand some key terms related to options trading:

- Premium: The price paid for purchasing an option.
- Strike Price: The price at which the underlying asset can be bought or sold.
- 3. Expiration Date: The last date on which the option can be exercised.
- In-the-Money: When an option has intrinsic value (a call option is in-the-money if the stock price is above the strike price; a put option is in-the-money if the stock price is below the strike price).
- Out-of-the-Money: When an option has no intrinsic value (a call option is out-of-the money if the stock price is below the strike price; a put option is out-of-the-money if the stock price is above the strike price).
- At-the-Money: When the stock price is equal to the strike price.

FUNDAMENTALS OF OPTIONS TRADING

Now that we understand the basic concepts and terminology, let's discuss the fundamental principles of trading options.

THE MECHANICS OF BUYING AND SELLING OPTIONS

When you buy a call option, you're purchasing the right to buy the underlying asset at the strike price before the expiration date. Conversely, when you buy a put option, you're purchasing the right to sell the underlying asset at the strike price before the expiration date.

However, you can also sell options. When you sell a call option, you take on the obligation to sell the underlying asset at the strike price, potentially requiring you to deliver the asset if the option is exercised. When you sell a put option, you take on the obligation to buy the underlying asset at the strike price, potentially requiring you to purchase the asset if the option is exercised.

DETERMINANTS OF OPTION TRADING

Several factors affect the price of an option, including:

1. Current Price of the Underlying Asset: The value of the underlying stock greatly influences the option premium.
2. Strike Price: The relationship between the strike price and the stock price affects whether the option is in-the-money or out-of-the-money.
3. Time to Expiration: The longer the time until expiration, the higher the premium, all else being equal, because more time allows for more potential movement in the stock price.
4. Volatility: Higher volatility increases the likelihood of the stock price moving significantly, thereby increasing the option's premium.
5. Interest Rates: Changes in interest rates can have a small impact on option prices.
6. Dividends: Expected dividends can impact option prices, particularly if the underlying asset pays out dividends before the option's expiration.

The Greeks

The Greeks are important metrics that help traders measure the risk and potential reward of an options position. The most common Greeks are Delta, Gamma, Theta, Vega, and Rho.

Delta

Delta measures the sensitivity of the option's price to a $1 change in the price of the underlying asset. For call options, Delta ranges from 0 to 1, while for put options, it ranges from -1 to 0.

Gamma

Gamma measures the rate of change in Delta for a $1 change in the stock price. High Gamma means Delta can change rapidly, indicating higher potential volatility.

Theta

Theta measures the rate at which an option's value declines as it approaches expiration, also known as time decay. Options lose value as time goes by, and Theta quantifies this effect.

Vega

Vega measures the sensitivity of the option's price to changes in the volatility of the underlying asset. Higher volatility increases an option's premium due to the greater potential for price swings.

Rho

Rho measures the sensitivity of the option's price to changes in interest rates. Although usually not as impactful as Delta, Gamma, Theta, and Vega, it is still a vital consideration in some market conditions.

BASIC OPTION STRATEGIES

With the foundational knowledge in place, let's explore some basic options trading strategies.

Buying Call Options

Buying call options is one of the simplest ways to start trading options. This strategy involves purchasing a call option to speculate that the price of the underlying asset will rise above the strike price before the option expires. This allows the investor to profit from the upside potential with limited risk—the most that can be lost is the premium paid for the option.

Example: Suppose you believe that Company XYZ, currently trading at $50, will increase in value. You might purchase a call option with a strike price of $55 that expires in three months. If the stock price rises above $55 before expiration, you can buy the stock at a discount and either sell it for a profit or hold onto it.

BUYING PUT OPTIONS

Buying put options allows investors to profit from a decline in the price of the underlying asset. This strategy involves purchasing a put option, which provides the right to sell the stock at the strike price, hedging against a drop in the asset's value.

Example: If you hold shares of Company A, currently trading at $80, and you worry the price might fall, you can purchase a put option with a strike price of $75. If the stock price falls below $75 before expiration, you can sell the stock at $75, thus protecting against the downside risk.

PROTECTIVE PUTS

A protective put strategy involves holding a long position in a stock while buying a put option for the same stock.

This provides downside protection without needing to sell the stock.

Example: Imagine you own shares of Company DEF, and its current price is $100. To protect your investment, you buy a put option with a strike price of $95. If the stock price falls, your losses will be limited to $95 minus the premium paid for the put option.

COVERED CALLS

A covered call strategy involves owning the underlying asset while selling a call option on the same asset. This can generate additional income from the option premium, potentially enhancing overall returns.

Day trading isn't governed by a specific rulebook, but there are some general principles that most successful day traders follow.

Stock trading involves navigating the often complex world of financial markets. Here are some principles to consider:

- Have a trading plan: Outline your strategy, including entry and exit points, risk management, and your capital allocation of your funds.
- Discipline is key: Stick to your plan and avoid emotional decisions. This is very difficult *

Manage risk: Always set up stop-loss orders to limit potential losses.

- Stay informed daily: research companies, follow market news, and be aware of economic data that can impact stock prices.
- Be patient: Successful trading often takes years, so take your time and gain experience.

HAVING A GOOD PLAN

- Develop a plan that outlines your entry and exit points, risk management techniques, and allocation of your capital.
- Risk Management: Always use stop-loss orders to limit your potential losses on every trade.
- Stay disciplined: Stick to your trading plan and avoid letting emotions influence your decisions.
- Be aware of the costs: Factor in commissions, margin interest, and other fees when calculating your potential profits.
- Do your research: Stay informed about the latest market news and economic data that could affect your trades.

TRADING STRATEGIES

Creating a trading strategy involves defining your approach to the market. Here's a general roadmap to get you started:

- Self-assessment: Consider your risk tolerance, available capital, and time commitment.
- Market selection: Choose a market (stocks, forex, etc.) that aligns with your interests and research capacity.
- Time frame: Decide on a timeframe for your trades (day trading, swing trading, etc.).
- Trading style: There are technical and fundamental analysis approaches. Explore which suits you better.
- Entry and exit triggers: Define rules for entering

and exiting trades based on your chosen analysis method.

- Risk management: Establish stop-loss levels to limit potential losses.
- Back testing: Test your strategy on historical data to assess its effectiveness.
- Refine and adapt: Continuously monitor and improve your strategy based on market conditions.

CONTROL EMOTIONS

Emotions can be a major obstacle in successful stock trading. Here's how to cultivate discipline and avoid letting emotions cloud your judgment:

- Plan your trades, trade your plan: Develop a trading strategy that outlines entry and exit points, and follow it rigorously.
- Acknowledge your emotions: Recognize emotional triggers like fear and greed and how they might influence your decisions.
- Take a step back: If emotions run high, take a break from trading to clear your head and regain composure.
- Focus on the process: Concentrate on executing your trading plan rather than the outcome of Absolutely. Sticking to your trading plan is crucial

for disciplined and successful trading. It helps you avoid emotional decisions and ensures consistency in your approach. Here are some reasons why following your trading plan is essential:

- Reduces emotional trading: The markets can be volatile, and emotions can cloud your judgment. A trading plan forces you to make decisions based on logic and analysis, not fear or greed.
- Improves discipline: A well-defined plan keeps you accountable and prevents impulsive actions.
- Provides a track record: By following your plan, you can track your performance and identify areas for improvement. individual trades.
- Practice mindfulness: Techniques like meditation can help you develop emotional awareness and detachment.

FINANCIAL NEWS

Here are some ways to stay informed about the latest market news and conduct research for trading:

- Financial news websites and apps: Renowned sources like Bloomberg, Reuters, CNBC, and Yahoo Finance provide up-to-date news, analysis, and market updates.
- Company filings and press releases: Stay on top of developments within specific companies you're

interested in by following their investor relations sections.

- Economic calendars: Monitor key economic data releases and events that can impact the market.
- Industry publications and research reports: Subscribe to newsletters or research reports from reputable financial institutions to gain deeper insights.
- Podcasts and webinars: Listen to podcasts and attend webinars hosted by financial experts for their analysis and perspectives.

TRADING JOURNAL

A trading journal is a valuable tool for tracking your trades, analyzing your performance, and identifying areas for improvement. Here's a basic guide to keeping a trading journal:

- Choose a format: Decide whether you prefer a physical notebook, a spreadsheet, or a dedicated trading journal app.
- Record key details: Track essential details like the date, asset traded, trade direction (long or short), entry and exit prices, and trade size.
- Capture your rationale: Briefly explain your reasoning behind each trade entry and exit.

- Track your emotions: Note your emotional state during each trade to identify potential biases.
- Review and reflect: Regularly analyze your trading journal entries to identify patterns, assess your strategy's effectiveness, and develop your trading discipline.

WHAT TIME TO TRADE

There's no single "best" time to trade stocks. Here's a breakdown of active trading times to consider:

- First hour (9:30 AM to 10:30 AM EST): This period often sees the biggest price movements, but volatility can be high.
- Last hour (3:00 PM to 4:00 PM EST): Activity picks up again as investors position themselves before the close.
- Avoid midday (11:30 AM to 2:30 PM EST): Trading tends to be quieter during lunch hours, potentially leading to lower liquidity and wider bid-ask spreads.

ONE TICKER

The number of trades for a beginner.

The number of trades for a beginner.

How many trades to make per week isn't as important as focusing on developing a solid trading plan and practicing discipline. Here's why:

- Focus on learning: Beginners should prioritize learning the ropes of trading rather than chasing frequent trades.
- Minimize risk: Frequent trading can increase exposure to potential losses, especially for beginners.
- Develop a strategy: A well-defined trading plan helps identify suitable trade opportunities and avoid impulsive decisions.

CASH OR MARGIN

Choosing between a cash account and a margin account depends on your experience and risk tolerance. Here's a quick comparison to help you decide:

- Cash Account: Suitable for beginners, focuses on buying stocks with available funds, minimizes risk.

- Margin Account: Allows borrowing money to amplify returns (and magnify losses), suitable for experienced traders comfortable with higher risk.

CANDLESTICK PATTERNS

Candlesticks patterns hold the key to understanding market sentiment and price action, making them an indispensable tool for traders seeking to make informed decisions. By gaining proficiency in reading them, you'll be better equipped to navigate the complex and ever-changing landscape of trading with precision and confidence. In this in-depth guide, the experts at TU will examine the top twenty best candlestick patterns that can significantly elevate your trading performance, covering the full spectrum from bullish and bearish patterns to those that signal reversals.

According to Traders Union's experts, the best candlestick patterns you should know for better trading include Bullish Engulfing, Bearish Engulfing, Hammer, Shooting Star, and Morning Star. These patterns encompass bullish, bearish, reversal, and continuation situations, allowing you to gain a deeper understanding of market movements and make well-informed trading decisions.

CANDLESTICKS

Candlestick charts are a popular way to visualize price movements in the financial markets. They offer a quick and informative way to see the open, high, low, and close prices for a given security over a specific period.

Here's a breakdown of the key elements of a candlestick:

- Body: The thick part of the candlestick represents the difference between the opening and closing prices. A filled body indicates a close higher (green) or lower (red) than the open.

- Wicks (or shadows): The thin lines extending from the top and bottom of the body represent the high and low prices for the period. A long upper wick shows the price reached above the close, while a long lower wick indicates the price dipped below the open.

The size and position of these elements can signal potential buying or selling pressure and provide clues about market sentiment. Remember, candlestick patterns should be used in conjunction with other technical indicators for a more comprehensive trading strategy.

A candlestick is a charting tool used in technical analysis to display the price movement of an asset, such as stocks, over a specific period of time. Each candlestick on a chart represents one unit of time (e.g., one day, one hour) and shows the opening, closing, high, and low prices for that period.

A typical candlestick consists of:

Body: The wider part of the candlestick represents the range between the opening and closing prices.

If the closing price is higher than the opening price, the body is typically filled or colored green or white.

If the closing price is lower than the opening price, the body is usually filled or colored red or black.

Wicks or Shadows: The thin lines above and below the body that represent the high and low prices during the period.

- The upper wick shows the highest price reached.
- The lower wick shows the lowest price reached.

Candlestick patterns are used to predict future price movements based on historical patterns. Some common patterns include:

- **Doji:** When the opening and closing prices are very close, resulting in a very small body, indicating indecision in the market.
- **Hammer:** A candlestick with a small body at the top and a long lower wick, suggesting a potential reversal from a downtrend to an uptrend.
- **Shooting Star:** A candlestick with a small body at the bottom and a long upper wick, indicating a potential reversal from an uptrend to a downtrend.

- **Engulfing:** When one candlestick's body completely engulfs the previous candlestick's body, signaling a potential reversal in the current trend.

These patterns, among others, help traders make decisions about buying or selling based on the visual representation of price movements and market sentiment.

WHAT TO TRADE

Among the three asset classes, stocks are generally considered the most popular for retail traders. This is likely due to several factors, including:

- Company familiarity: Many investors are more familiar with publicly traded companies and their products or services compared to the intricacies of currency markets or futures contracts.
- Accessibility: Stock trading platforms tend to be user-friendly and have lower minimum investment requirements compared to futures trading.
- Investment opportunities: Stocks offer the potential for capital appreciation through dividends and stock price increases, while forex and futures are primarily for speculation on price movements.

TECHNICAL ANALYSIS

Technical analysis is a method used in finance to predict the direction of prices by studying historical market data, primarily price and volume. Technical analysts believe that past trading activity can be a valuable indicator of future price movements. They use charts and technical indicators to identify trends and patterns in the data.

Technical analysis is a complex subject, but it can be a useful tool for investors who want to learn more about how markets work. However, it's important to remember that technical analysis is not a foolproof way to predict the future. The markets are constantly changing, and there is no guarantee that past patterns will continue to hold true.

TECHNICAL INDICATORS

Technical indicators are mathematical calculations used in technical analysis to analyze price, volume, and momentum data in order to identify trading opportunities. They are tools that help traders interpret the financial markets and potentially forecast future price movements. There are many different types of technical indicators, each with its own strengths and weaknesses. Some of the most common technical indicators include:

- Moving averages: Moving averages are a simple way to smooth out price data and identify trends.
- Relative Strength Index (RSI): The RSI is a popular oscillator that measures the relative strength or weakness of a price movement.
- Moving Average Convergence Divergence (MACD): The MACD is a trend-following momentum indicator that shows the relationship between two moving averages of a security's price.
- Bollinger Bands: Bollinger Bands are a volatility indicator that shows the upper and lower bands of a security's price based on its historical volatility.

These are just a few examples of the many technical indicators that are available to traders. It is important to understand how each indicator works before using it in your trading.

DISCIPLINE

Sticking to your trading plan is crucial for disciplined and successful trading. It helps you avoid emotional decisions and ensures consistency in your approach. Here are some reasons why following your trading plan is essential:

- Reduces emotional trading: The markets can be volatile, and emotions can cloud your judgment. A trading plan forces you to make decisions based on logic and analysis, not fear or greed.
- Improves discipline: A well-defined plan keeps you accountable and prevents impulsive actions.
- Provides a track record: By following your plan, you can track your performance and identify areas for improvement.

TOOLS FOR TRADING

Day trading requires a combination of tools to analyze market data, execute trades quickly, and manage risk effectively. Here are some of the best tools commonly used by day traders:

Trading Platforms

1. Thinkorswim by TD Ameritrade: Offers advanced charting tools, technical analysis, and a variety of trading instruments.
2. MetaTrader 4 (MT4) & MetaTrader 5 (MT5): Popular platforms with extensive charting capabilities, custom indicators, and automated trading features.

3. TradeStation: Known for its powerful analytical tools, customizable trading strategies, and direct market access.
4. Interactive Brokers (IBKR): Offers a robust trading platform with extensive research tools and low-cost trading.

Charting Tools

1. TradingView: Provides advanced charting capabilities, social networking features, and access to a wide range of markets.
2. StockCharts: Easy-to-use charting tool with a variety of technical indicators and realtime data.
3. NinjaTrader: Focuses on advanced charting, market analytics, and trade simulation.

Scanners and Screeners

1. Finviz: Offers powerful stock screening, heat maps, and market news.
2. Trade Ideas: Use AI to provide stock screening, backtesting, and real-time alerts.

BUY
SELL

STOP LOSS

A stop-loss order is an instruction placed with a broker to automatically buy or sell a security when it reaches a certain price, helping to limit potential losses in the investment. It's a helpful tool for managing risk, especially for new investors.

HOW STOP-LOSS ORDERS WORK

Traders or investors may choose to use a stop-loss order to limit their losses and protect their profits. By placing a stop-loss order, they can manage risk by exiting a position if the price for their security starts moving in the direction opposite to the position they have taken.

KEY TAKEAWAYS

A stop-loss order instructs that a stock be bought or sold when it reaches a specified price known as the stop price.

Once the stop price is met, the stop order becomes a market order and is executed at the next available opportunity.

Stop-loss orders are used to limit loss or lock in profit on existing positions.

They can protect investors with either long or short positions.

A stop-loss order is different from a stop-limit order, the latter of which must be executed at a specific price rather than at the market.

RISK MANAGEMENT

Risk management is essential for any stock trader, regardless of experience level. It's a set of practices that helps you minimize potential losses and protect your capital. Here are some key risk management strategies for stock trading:

- Position Sizing: Limit the amount of capital you risk on any single trade. A common approach is the

1% rule, which suggests risking no more than 1% of your account value per trade.

- Stop-Loss Orders: A stop-loss order automatically exits your position if the stock price falls below a certain level, limiting your losses.
- Take-Profit Orders: A take-profit order helps you lock in gains by automatically selling your shares when the stock price reaches a target level.
- Risk-Reward Ratio: This ratio compares your potential profit to your potential loss on a trade. Aim for trades with a higher reward than risk.
- Diversification: Spread your investments across different stocks and sectors to reduce your exposure to any single company or industry.
- Discipline: Sticking to your trading plan and avoiding emotional decisions is crucial for risk management.

GME
GameStop
$321.00
WHAT IS
Volatility?

VOLATILITY

Volatility in trading refers to the rate at which the price of an asset fluctuates over time. High volatility indicates significant price swings, up or down, within a short period. Low volatility suggests prices move slowly and remain relatively stable.

Volatility is a key factor for traders to consider, as it can impact both risk and reward potential. Here's a breakdown of how volatility affects trading:

- Higher Volatility: Offers increased profit potential but also amplifies potential losses. Requires strong risk management strategies.
- Lower Volatility: Presents lower risk but also generally translates to lower potential returns.

TYPES OF TRADING

There are two main ways to categorize trading styles: by time horizon and by trading strategy.

- Time horizon refers to how long a trader holds a position before buying or selling. Common time horizons include:
- Scalping: Positions are held for seconds or minutes.
- Day trading: Positions are held for a single trading day.
- Swing trading: Positions are held for several days to weeks.
- Position trading: Positions are held for months or even years.
- Trading strategy refers to the specific method a trader uses to identify trading opportunities. Some common trading strategies include:

- Trend following: Capitalizing on prevailing market trends.
- Range trading: Profiting from price fluctuations within a specific range.
- Mean reversion: Trading on the expectation that prices will eventually revert to their historical averages.
- Breakout trading: Benefiting from asset prices breaking above resistance levels or below support levels.
- Momentum trading: Riding out strong price movements.

COMMON TYPES OF TRADING STRATEGIES

Yes, these are common types of trading strategies. Here's a brief overview of each:

1. Intraday Trading:

- Description: Trades are executed within the same trading day. Positions are opened and closed on the same day.
- Goal: To capitalize on small price movements within a single day.
- Timeframe: Minutes to hours.

2. Positional Trading:

- Description: Trades are held for weeks to months.
- Goal: To take advantage of longer-term trends without the need to monitor the market constantly.
- Timeframe: Weeks to months.

3. Swing Trading:

- Description: Trades are held for several days to a few weeks.
- Goal: To profit from short- to medium-term price swings in the market.
- Timeframe: Days to weeks.

4. Long-Term Trading:

- Description: Investments are held for several months to years.
- Goal: To benefit from long-term growth and trends.
- Timeframe: Months to years.

5. Scalping:

- Description: Involves making dozens or hundreds of trades in a day, holding positions for very short periods (seconds to minutes).
- Goal: To achieve small profits on each trade, which accumulate over time.
- Timeframe: Seconds to minutes.

6. Momentum Trading:

- Description: Involves trading in the direction of strong price movements (upward or downward).
- Goal: To capitalize on market volatility and momentum.
- Timeframe: Varies, can range from minutes to days.

Each trading strategy requires different skills, risk management techniques, and time commitments. Traders often choose the strategy that best fits their personality, time availability, and financial goals.

TYPES OF TRADING IN STOCK MARKET

BUY AND SELL A STOCK WITH IN ONE MINUTE	SCALPING
BUY AND SELL A STOCK WITH IN ONE DAY	DAY TRADING
BUY AND SELL A STOCK WITH IN ONE WEEK	SWING TRADING
BUY AND SELL A STOCK WITH IN ONE MONTH	TREND TRADING
BUY AND SELL A STOCK WITH IN ONE YEAR	POSITIONAL TRADING
BUY AND HOLD A STOCK FOR MANY YEARS	INVESTING

TECHNICAL ANALYSIS

Technical analysis is a method used by investors and traders to evaluate investments and identify trading opportunities by analyzing statistical trends gathered from trading activity, such as price movement and volume. Technical analysts believe that past trading activity and price changes of a security can be valuable indicators of the security's future price movements. It's essentially using historical data to forecast future market behavior.

KEY TAKEAWAYS

Technical analysis is a trading discipline.

- Technical analysts believe past trading activity and price changes of a security can be valuable indicators of the security's future price movements.

- Technical analysis may be contrasted with fundamental analysis, which focuses on a company's financials rather than historical price patterns or stock trends.

TRADING

Trading stocks can be both fascinating and lucrative, but it's essential to approach it with the right knowledge and mindset. Here are six essential steps to get started in stock trading:

Decide Your Trading Style: Consider your personality, risk tolerance, and time commitment.

Are you interested in short-term day trading or longer-term swing or position trading? Choose a style that aligns with your goals and abilities.

Research Brokerages: Look for a brokerage platform that suits your trading style. Ensure it offers the tools, resources, and support you need.

Open a Brokerage Account: Once you've chosen a brokerage, open an account and fund it. This will be your gateway to the stock market.

Research Stocks: Examine stocks you want to trade using fundamental and technical analysis. Understand the companies, their financials, and market trends.

Place Your Orders: Learn about different order types (e.g., market orders, limit orders) and their risks and advantages. Place orders to buy or sell stocks based on your analysis.

Manage Risk: Create a strong risk management plan. This includes proper position sizing, setting stop-loss orders, and diversifying your investments.

Remember, continuous learning and expanding your knowledge will help you thrive in the ever-changing stock market

CRYPTOCURRENCY TRADING

Cryptocurrency trading is gaining momentum among retail traders. There are thousands of digital coins available and a vast choice of exchanges, platforms, and resources on how to trade these digital assets.

What is Crypto Trading?

With a high risk of losing money rapidly due to leverage. 75% of retail investor accounts lose money when trading

CFDs with this provider. You should consider whether you understand how CFDs work and whether you can afford to take the high risk of losing.

Cryptocurrency trading is gaining momentum among retail traders. There are thousands of digital coins available and a vast choice of exchanges, platforms and resources on how to trade these digital assets.

No table of figures entries found.

What is crypto trading exactly, and how can you start your journey?

In this guide, we answer some of the pressing questions you may have, from what moves cryptocurrency markets to what tradable instruments and strategies are available, and more.

What is Cryptocurrency Trading?

Cryptocurrency trading is speculating on the price of cryptocurrencies against the US dollar and other fiat currencies, or against other crypto currencies, in an attempt to benefit from their highly volatile fluctuations. Increased volatility makes cryptocurrencies risky. Their price can move suddenly against your trade, causing losses.

Crypto trading may also mean buying and selling derivatives to speculate on price fluctuations.

A cryptocurrency is a decentralized digital currency. It works through a system of peer-to peer (P2P) transaction checks, with no central server. As cryptocurrencies run on decentralized computer networks, they are not issued or controlled by a central authority.

Currency trading is different from cryptocurrency trading, meaning that cryptocurrencies differ from fiat currencies such as the British pound sterling (GBP) or US dollar (USD). A fiat currency is issued by a government and guaranteed and controlled by a central bank.

ALGORITHMIC TRADING

Algorithmic trading, often referred to as algo trading, is the use of computer algorithms to execute trades in financial markets. These algorithms make decisions about the timing, price, and quantity of trades based on predefined criteria and statistical models. Here's a brief overview of key aspects:

Automation: Algorithms automatically place trades, reducing the need for human intervention and enabling faster execution.

Strategies: Common strategies include arbitrage (exploiting price differences between markets), trend following (buying or selling based on market momentum), and market making (providing liquidity by placing both buy and sell orders).

Speed and Efficiency: Algorithms can analyze vast amounts of data quickly, identifying trading opportunities and executing trades in milliseconds.

Risk Management: Algorithms can include risk management rules, such as stop-loss orders, to minimize potential losses.

High-Frequency Trading (HFT): A subset of algorithmic trading that involves making a large number of trades in extremely short time frames to capitalize on small price discrepancies.

Overall, algorithmic trading aims to improve trading performance by leveraging speed, precision, and advanced data analysis.

THE RIGHT STOCKS

Choosing the right stocks to trade involves a combination of research, analysis, and strategy. Here are some key steps to help you make informed decisions:

#1. Understand Your Goals and Risk Tolerance

- Define Your Objectives: Are you looking for short-term gains, long-term investments, or a combination?
- Assess Your Risk Tolerance: How much risk are you willing to take? This will influence whether you choose volatile stocks or more stable ones.

#2. Conduct Fundamental Analysis

- Company Financials: Look at earnings reports, revenue growth, profit margins, and debt levels.
- Valuation Metrics: Use ratios like Price-to-Earnings (P/E), Price-to-Sales (P/S), and Price to-Book (P/B) to assess if a stock is undervalued or overvalued.
- Industry Position: Consider the company's market share, competitive advantages, and industry trends.

#3. Perform Technical Analysis

- Price Trends: Analyze historical price movements and identify patterns such as support and resistance levels.
- Indicators: Use tools like Moving Averages, Relative Strength Index (RSI), and Bollinger Bands to gain insights into stock momentum and potential turning points.
- Volume Analysis: High trading volumes can indicate strong interest and potential price movement.

#4. Consider Market Conditions

- Economic Indicators: Pay attention to economic

data such as GDP growth, unemployment rates, and inflation.

- Interest Rates: Changes in interest rates can significantly impact stock prices.
- Global Events: Geopolitical events, trade policies, and other global factors can influence market sentiment.

#5. Follow News and Developments

- Stay Updated: Regularly read financial news, company announcements, and earnings reports.
- Sector News: Some sectors may outperform others based on technological advancements, regulatory changes, or consumer trends.

#6. Use Stock Screeners

- Screen for Criteria: Use online tools to filter stocks based on specific criteria like market capitalization, dividend yield, and earnings growth.
- Custom Screens: Create custom screens that match your investment strategy.

#7. Diversify Your Portfolio

- Spread Risk: Don't put all your money into one stock or sector. Diversify to mitigate risk.

- Balance Types: Consider a mix of growth stocks, dividend stocks, and defensive stocks.

#8. Evaluate Management and Corporate Governance

- Leadership Quality: Research the company's leadership team and their track record.
- Corporate Governance: Ensure the company has strong governance practices and ethical standards.

#9. Monitor and Review

- Regular Reviews: Continuously monitor your portfolio and review your positions.
- Adjust Strategies: Be prepared to adjust your strategies based on market conditions and performance.

#10. Seek Expert Advice

- Financial Advisors: Consider consulting with financial advisors or using reputable research reports for guidance.
- Educational Resources: Take advantage of online courses, webinars, and books on stock trading and investment strategies.

By combining these approaches, you can make more informed decisions and increase your chances of success in the stock market.

TIMELINE

Trading times for stock markets can vary based on the country and specific market. Here are the standard trading hours for some of the major stock exchanges:

1. New York Stock Exchange (NYSE) and NASDAQ (USA)

- Regular Trading Hours: Monday to Friday, 9:30 AM to 4:00 PM (Eastern Time, ET)
- Pre-Market Hours: 4:00 AM to 9:30 AM (ET)
- After-Hours Trading: 4:00 PM to 8:00 PM (ET)

2. London Stock Exchange (LSE)

- Regular Trading Hours: Monday to Friday, 8:00 AM to 4:30 PM (Greenwich Mean Time, GMT)

3. Tokyo Stock Exchange (TSE)

- Regular Trading Hours: Monday to Friday, 9:00

AM to 11:30 AM and 12:30 PM to 3:00 PM (Japan Standard Time, JST)

4. Shanghai Stock Exchange (SSE)

- Regular Trading Hours: Monday to Friday, 9:30 AM to 11:30 AM and 1:00 PM to 3:00 PM (China Standard Time, CST)

5. Hong Kong Stock Exchange (HKEX)

- Regular Trading Hours: Monday to Friday, 9:30 AM to 12:00 PM and 1:00 PM to 4:00 PM (Hong Kong Time, HKT)

6. Euronext (various European countries including France, Netherlands, and Belgium)

- Regular Trading Hours: Monday to Friday, 9:00 AM to 5:30 PM (Central European Time, CET)

7. Australian Securities Exchange (ASX)

- Regular Trading Hours: Monday to Friday, 10:00 AM to 4:00 PM (Australian Eastern Standard Time, AEST)

These hours can be subject to change on holidays or during special circumstances. Additionally, some markets may offer extended trading hours or have specific times for different types of trades. Always check with the specific exchange for the most accurate and up-to-date information.

MAKING TRADING SIMPLE

It involves a few key principles that can help streamline the process and make it more accessible.

- Educate Yourself: Understand the basics of trading, including key terms, market mechanisms, and different types of assets. Resources like books, online courses, and financial news can be valuable.

- Develop a Strategy: Decide on a trading strategy that fits your goals and risk tolerance. Popular strategies include day trading, swing trading, and long-term investing. Stick to your strategy and avoid making impulsive decisions.

- Use Simple Tools: Utilize trading platforms that offer intuitive interfaces and essential tools without over-whelming features. Many platforms provide educational resources and demo accounts for practice.

- Set Clear Goals: Define what you want to achieve with trading. Set specific, measurable, achievable, relevant, and time-bound (SMART) goals to stay focused.

- Manage Risk: Implement risk management techniques such as stop-loss orders and position sizing to protect your capital. Never invest more than you can afford to lose.

- Stay Informed: Keep up with market news and trends but avoid information overload. Follow a few reliable sources and focus on relevant information for your strategy.

- Track and Review: Maintain a trading journal to track your trades, decisions, and outcomes. Regularly review your performance to identify strengths and areas for improvement.

By following these principles, you can simplify your trading approach, making it more manageable and potentially more successful.

DIVIDEND STOCKS

Dividend Stocks are shares of companies that regularly distribute a portion of their earnings to shareholders in the form of dividends.

These dividends are typically paid on a quarterly basis, though some companies may distribute them monthly, semi-annually, or annually.

Investing in dividend stocks can provide a steady income stream and potential for capital appreciation. These stocks are often considered a good choice for income-focused investors, such as retirees, because they offer regular payments. Dividend stocks are typically found in more established, financially stable companies that have a history of profitability and consistent earnings.

Key Points about Dividend Stocks:

1. Regular Income: Dividends provide a consistent source of income, which can be especially appealing for income-seeking investors.
2. Types of Dividends: Dividends can be paid in cash or additional shares of stock.
3. Dividend Yield: This is a key metric, calculated as the annual dividend payment divided by the stock's current price. It helps investors gauge the return on investment from dividends alone.
4. Reinvestment: Many investors choose to reinvest dividends to purchase more shares, which can compound returns over time.
5. Stability and Growth: Dividend-paying companies are often mature and stable, and the dividends can indicate strong financial health and a positive outlook on future earnings.
6. Tax Considerations: Dividends are subject to taxation, but qualified dividends in the U.S. are typically taxed at a lower rate than regular income.

Examples of Dividend Stocks:

- Blue-chip stocks:Large, well-established companies with a history of reliable performance, like Coca-Cola, Johnson & Johnson, and Procter & Gamble.
- Real Estate Investment Trusts (REITs): These often pay higher-than-average dividends due to their structure and tax requirements.

Investing in dividend stocks can be a good strategy for those looking for a balance of income and growth, providing both regular payments and the potential for share price appreciation.

ANALYZING STOCKS

Picking and analyzing stocks involves a combination of qualitative and quantitative analysis. Here's a step-by-step guide to help you get started:

Understand Your Investment Goals and Risk Tolerance

Before selecting stocks, define your investment goals (e.g., growth, income, value) and understand your risk tolerance (how much risk you can handle without panic).

Fundamental Analysis

This involves analyzing a company's financial health and performance. Key steps include:

A. Financial Statements

- Income Statement: Look at revenue, expenses, and profits over time.
- Balance Sheet: Examine assets, liabilities, and shareholder equity.

- Cash Flow Statement: Assess the cash inflows and outflows from operations, investing, and financing.

B. Key Financial Ratios

- Price-to-Earnings (P/E) Ratio: Evaluates the company's current share price relative to its per-share earnings.
- Price-to-Book (P/B) Ratio: Compares the market value of a company to its book value.
- Debt-to-Equity (D/E) Ratio: Assesses a company's financial leverage by comparing its total liabilities to shareholders' equity.
- Return on Equity (ROE): Measures profitability by showing how much profit a company generates with the money shareholders have invested.

C. Growth Indicators

- Revenue Growth: Consistent revenue growth is a good sign of a healthy business.
- Earnings Growth: Look for companies with consistent and strong earnings growth.

D. Dividends

- Dividend Yield: Percentage of the current stock price paid out in dividends annually.

- Payout Ratio: The proportion of earnings paid out as dividends.

E. Qualitative Analysis

Consider non-numerical aspects that might impact the stock's performance:

- Management Quality: Research the track record and experience of the company's management team.
- Industry Position: Understand the company's position within its industry. Is it a market leader?
- Competitive Advantage: Identify any sustainable competitive advantages (moats), such as strong brand recognition

TRADING SCHOOLS

Here are some of the top trading schools for 2024, each offering unique strengths and specialties:

- Investors Underground: Known for its comprehensive and high-quality courses like

Textbook Trading and Tandem Trader, Investors Underground is a top choice for those looking to dive deep into stock trading with the guidance of experienced trader. However, it is on the pricier side

- Warrior Trading: Founded by Ross Cameron, Warrior Trading offers robust educational resources, including a highly rated chat room and real-time trading simulator. It provides courses tailored to different levels, from beginners to advanced traders, and emphasizes a solid curriculum and mentorship

- Bulls on Wall Street: This school offers a 60-day bootcamp focused on practical, live trading sessions. Led by Kunal Desai, it is ideal for beginners and intermediates looking for an interactive and structured learning environment. The course includes a blend of theoretical learning and hands-on trading practice

- Mindful Trader: This platform offers a data-driven approach to trading, created by Stanford graduate Eric, who spent years developing a statistically backed trading strategy. It combines stock picks and educational content for a flat monthly fee, making it a good option for those interested in quantitative trading strategies

- Silvia Bellrock: The Bellrock Accelerator: Aimed primarily at beginners and intermediates, this course focuses on technical analysis and risk management. It offers lifetime access to materials, regular updates, and opportunities for personalized advice

- Bullish Bears: This course is praised for its value, offering comprehensive resources for just $47 per month. It includes live-streaming trading rooms, a supportive community, and a wide range of educational materials, although it lacks a trading simulator

- Timothy Sykes Trading Program: Specializing in penny stocks, this program is led by one of the top penny stock traders. While it offers a variety of educational materials and a chatroom, its flashy marketing style and lack of transparent pricing may not appeal to everyone

Each of these schools offers a different approach and set of resources, so the best choice depends on your specific needs, budget, and trading goals.

FUTURES TRADING

Futures trading involves buying and selling futures contracts, which are standardized agreements to buy or sell a specific quantity of an asset at a predetermined price at a specified future date. Here's a brief overview:

- Purpose: Futures contracts are used for hedging or speculation. Hedgers use futures to protect against price changes, while speculators aim to profit from price movements.

- Assets: Futures contracts can be based on a variety of underlying assets, including commodities (like oil, gold, and wheat), financial instruments (such as currencies, interest rates, and stock indexes), and even cryptocurrencies.

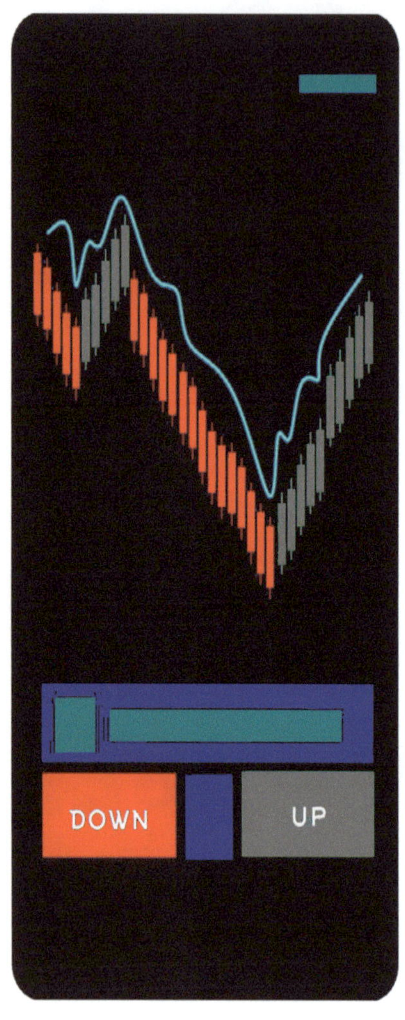

- Leverage: Futures trading often involves leverage, allowing traders to control large positions with a relatively small amount of capital. This amplifies both potential gains and losses.

- Standardization: Futures contracts are standardized in terms of quantity, quality, and delivery time, which facilitates trading on futures exchanges.

- Margin: Traders are required to deposit an initial margin (a fraction of the contract's value) to open a position and maintain a minimum margin level throughout the trade. If the market moves against their position, they might receive a margin call to add more funds.

- Expiration: Each futures contract has a specified expiration date. Traders can either close their positions before expiration or, in some cases, take or make delivery of the underlying asset.

Settlement: Futures contracts can be settled in two ways:

- Physical delivery: The actual asset is delivered upon contract expiration.
- Cash settlement: The difference between the contract price and the market price at expiration is settled in cash.

Market Participants:

- Hedgers: Use futures to mitigate the risk of price changes in the underlying asset.
- Speculators: Aim to profit from market price movements.
- Arbitrageurs: Seek to profit from price discrepancies between different markets or related assets.

Risk Management:

Futures trading is risky due to leverage and market volatility. Traders use various risk management techniques, such as stop-loss orders and diversification, to mitigate these risks.

Regulation:

Futures markets are regulated by governmental bodies (like the Commodity Futures Trading Commission in the U.S.) to ensure fair trading practices and protect market participants.

FOREX

Forex, short for "foreign exchange," refers to the global marketplace for buying and selling currencies. It is one of the largest and most liquid financial markets in the world, with a daily trading volume exceeding $6 trillion.

Here are points about Forex:

- Currency Pairs: Forex trading involves currency pairs, such as EUR/USD, GBP/JPY, and USD/JPY. Each pair represents the exchange rate between two currencies.

- Market Participants: Participants in the Forex market include banks, financial institutions, corporations, governments, and individual traders.

- Trading Hours: The Forex market operates twenty-four hours a day, five days a week, allowing for continuous trading across different time zones.

- Leverage and Margin: Forex trading often involves the use of leverage, which allows traders to control large positions with a relatively small amount of capital. However, leverage can also amplify losses.

- Market Influences: Factors influencing the Forex market include economic data, interest rates, political events, and market sentiment.

- Technical and Fundamental Analysis: Traders use various strategies to analyze the market, including technical analysis (studying price charts and patterns) and fundamental analysis (assessing economic indicators and news).

CFDS

Contracts for Difference (CFDs) are financial derivatives that allow traders to speculate on the price movements of various assets without actually owning the underlying asset. Here's a brief overview:

Key Features of CFDs:

1. Speculation on Price Movements:

- Traders can profit from both rising and falling markets.
- If you think the price of an asset will go up, you can buy (go long).
- If you think the price will go down, you can sell (go short).

2. Leverage:

- CFDs are typically traded on margin, meaning you can open a position with a fraction of the total trade value.
- This magnifies potential gains but also increases potential losses.

3. No Ownership:

- When trading CFDs, you don't own the underlying asset, such as shares, commodities, or currencies.

4. Diverse Range of Markets:

- CFDs can be used to trade a variety of financial instruments, including stocks, indices, commodities, currencies, and cryptocurrencies.

5. Cost:

- Traders pay the spread (the difference between the buy and sell price).
- There may also be other fees, such as overnight financing charges if positions are held overnight.

Advantages:

- Flexibility: Access to a wide range of markets and assets.
- Leverage: Potential to amplify returns.
- Hedging: Can be used to hedge against potential losses in an existing portfolio.

Risks:

Leverage Risk: Amplified losses as well as gains.

- Market Risk: Prices can move quickly, leading to significant losses.
- Counterparty Risk: Dependence on the CFD provider's financial health.

Example:

Suppose you believe the stock price of Company XYZ, currently at $100, will increase. You buy a CFD for 100 shares. If the price rises to $110, you make a profit of $10 per share (total profit $1,000).

REVIEW

Option trading involves buying and selling options, which are financial instruments that give you the right, but not the obligation, to buy or sell an underlying asset at a predetermined price before a specific date. Here are the basic steps to get started with option trading:

1. Understand the Basics

- Option Types: There are two types of options: calls (the right to buy) and puts (the right to sell).
- Strike Price: The price at which the underlying asset can be bought or sold.
- Expiration Date: The date by which the option must be exercised or it expires worthless.
- Premium: The price you pay to buy the option.

. . .

2. Learn Key Concepts

- Intrinsic Value: The difference between the underlying asset's price and the strike price.
- Time Value: The additional value of an option based on the time remaining until expiration.
- In-the-Money (ITM): An option with intrinsic value.
- Out-of-the-Money (OTM): An option without intrinsic value.
- At-the-Money (ATM): An option with a strike price close to the current price of the underlying asset.

3. Choose a Brokerage

Select a brokerage that supports option trading and offers tools and resources for beginners. Popular options include:

- TD Ameritrade
- E*TRADE
- Robinhood
- Fidelity

4. Develop a Strategy

Some common strategies include:

- Buying Calls: You expect the underlying asset's price to rise.
- Buying Puts: You expect the underlying asset's price to fall.
- Covered Calls: Owning the underlying asset and selling call options against it to generate income.
- Protective Puts: Buying puts to protect against a decline in the price of an asset you own.

5. Practice with a Paper Trading Account

Many brokerages offer paper trading accounts where you can practice without risking real money.

- **Start Small**

Begin with simple strategies and small positions. As you gain experience, you can explore more complex strategies and larger positions.

- **Monitor and Manage Your Trades**

Keep an eye on your positions and the market. Be prepared to adjust your strategy or close positions as needed.

- **Continue Learning**

Option trading is complex and requires ongoing education. Utilize online resources, books, and courses to deepen your understanding.

Would you like detailed examples of specific option strategies or any other information?

SPECIFIC OPTION STRATEGIES

Detailed Examples of Specific Option Strategies:

Momentum Trading

- Description: Buying securities that have shown an upward trend and selling those with downward trends.
- Objective: Capture gains from market momentum.
- Key Features: Relies on the strength of price trends and trading volumes.

News-Based Trading

- Description: Making trading decisions based on news announcements and events.
- Objective: Take advantage of market reactions to news.
- Key Features: Requires quick response to news and market developments.

Pairs Trading

- Description: Taking long and short positions in two correlated securities.
- Objective: Profit from the relative performance of the two securities.
- Key Features: Market-neutral strategy, relies on statistical analysis.

Options Trading

- Description: Trading options contracts rather than the underlying securities.
- Objective: Leverage positions and hedge risk.
- Key Features: Involves strategies like calls, puts, spreads, and straddles.

Value Investing

- Description: Buying undervalued stocks with strong fundamentals.
- Objective: Long-term capital appreciation.
- Key Features: Focus on intrinsic value and fundamental analysis.

Growth Investing

- Description: Investing in companies with strong potential for growth.
- Objective: Capitalize on future growth prospects.
- Key Features: Emphasis on earnings growth, revenue growth, and expansion potential.

These strategies can be applied individually or in combination, depending on the trader's goals, risk tolerance, and market conditions.

Here are detailed examples of a few common option strategies:

- **Buying Calls Objective:** Profit from a rise in the underlying asset's price.

Example: You buy a call option for Stock ABC with a strike price of $50, expiring in one month, for a premium of $2.

- If Stock ABC rises to $60, you can exercise your option to buy at $50 and sell at $60, making a profit (ignoring the premium for simplicity). If the stock stays below $50, your maximum loss is the premium paid ($2).

- **Buying Puts Objective:** Profit from a decline in the underlying asset's price. Example: You buy a put option for Stock XYZ with a strike price of $30, expiring in one month, for a premium of $1.50.

- If Stock XYZ falls to $20, you can exercise your option to sell at $30 and then buy at $20, making a profit (ignoring the premium). If the stock stays above $30, your maximum loss is the premium paid ($1.50).

- **Covered Calls Objective:** Generate additional income from an existing stock position. Example: You own 100 shares of Stock DEF, currently trading at $40. You sell a call option with a strike price of $45, expiring in one month, for a premium of $1.

- If Stock DEF stays below $45, you keep the premium ($1) as income. If the stock rises above $45, you might have to sell your shares at $45, but you still keep the premium, effectively selling your shares at $46 ($45 + $1).

- **Protective Puts Objective:** Protect against a decline in the price of an asset you own. Example: You own 100 shares of Stock GHI, currently trading at $60. You buy a put option with a strike price of $55, expiring in one month, for a premium of $2.

- Scenario: If Stock GHI falls to $50, you can sell your shares at $55, limiting your loss to $5 per share plus the premium ($2). If the stock stays above $55, your maximum loss is the premium paid ($2).

- **Straddle Objective:** Profit from significant movement in the underlying asset's price, regardless of direction.

- Objective: Profit from low volatility and range-bound movement. These examples illustrate some basic strategies. Each has its own risk-reward profile and understanding them deeply requires practice and continuous learning.

CONTINUE LEARNING
EFFECTIVELY

Day trading can be complex but rewarding. Here are steps to help you continue learning effectively:

1. Build a Strong Foundation:

- Read Books: Start with classic day trading books

  - Day Trading for Dummies
  - A Beginner's Guide to Day Trading Online

- Online Courses: Enroll in courses from platforms like Udemy, Coursera, or Investopedia Academy.

- Learn the basics.

. . .

2. Stay Updated with Market News:

- Financial News Websites Regularly read sites like Bloomberg, CNBC, and MarketWatch.

- News Apps: Use apps like Yahoo Finance or Investing.com for real-time updates.

3. Join Trading Communities:

- Forums: Participate in forums like Day trading on Reddit or Elite Trader.

- Social Media: Follow experienced traders on Twitter and join trading groups on Facebook.

4. Use Simulation Tools:

- Paper Trading: Use platforms like ThinkorSwim by TD Ameritrade or TradingView to practice without real money.

- Back testing Test your strategies on historical data.

5. Develop a Trading Plan:

- Set Goals: Define your financial goals and risk tolerance.

- Establish Rules: Create rules for entry and exit points, stop losses, and position sizing.

6. Focus on Risk Management:

- Stop Loss Orders and Always use stop loss to limit potential losses.

- Position Sizing- Only risk a small percentage of your capital on each trade.

7. Analyze Your Trades

- Trading Journal: Keep a detailed journal of all your trades to analyze and learn from your mistakes.

- Performance Reviews: Regularly review your trading performance to adjust strategies as needed.

8. Stay Disciplined and Patient:

- Emotional Control: Learn to manage emotions and stick to your trading plan.

- Continuous Learning: Markets evolve, so keep learning and adapting your strategies.

By following these steps, you can build a solid foundation and continue to improve your day trading skills.

Supply and Demand

Supply and demand in stock trading are fundamental concepts that determine the price of stocks. Here's a breakdown of how they work:

- Supply: This refers to the number of shares available for sale at various price levels. When there are more shares available than buyers, the supply exceeds demand, leading to a decrease in the stock price.

- Demand: This refers to the number of shares investors want to buy at different price levels. When more investors want to buy shares than there are shares available for sale, the demand exceeds supply, causing the stock price to rise

The interaction between supply and demand influences stock prices continuously. If demand increases (more buyers) or supply decreases (fewer sellers), stock prices generally rise. Conversely, if demand decreases (fewer buyers) or supply increases (more sellers), stock prices tend to fall. This balance is what traders and investors constantly analyze to make informed trading decisions.

Auto trading involves using software to automate the trading process in financial markets. Here are some steps to get started:

- Choose a Market: Decide whether you want to trade stocks, forex, crypto currencies, or another asset class.

- Select a Trading Platform: Platforms like MetaTrader 4/5, TradingView, or brokerage specific platforms often support auto trading.

- Develop or Buy a Trading Bot:

Develop: If you have programming skills, you can develop your own bot using languages like Python, MQL4/5, or others.

Buy: There are many commercial bots available. Be sure to research and choose a reputable one.

- Back test the Strategy: Use historical data to test the performance of your trading bot to ensure it is profitable.

- Set Up the Bot: Configure the bot with your chosen platform, input your trading parameters, and ensure it is working correctly.

- Monitor and Adjust: Regularly monitor the bot's performance and make necessary adjustments to optimize its performance.

5 TRADING RULES I FOLLOW

1. Stick to the plan you created, take classes to educate yourself

2. Trade one or two tickers, risk a small percentage

3. Watch news before trading and understand the risk

4. Have a exit plan and manage risk

5. Control your emotions, set stop loss